Learning Tree
1 2 3

A to Z

By Deborah Manley
Illustrated by Joanne Flindall

**Geddes+
Grosset**

Read this book and see if you can answer the questions. Ask an adult or an older friend to tell you if your answers are right or to help you if you find the questions difficult. Often there is more than one answer to a question.

First published in hardback 1990
Copyright © Cherrytree Press Ltd 1990

This paperback edition first published 1991 by
Geddes & Grosset Ltd
David Dale House
New Lanark ML11 9DJ

ISBN 1 85534 454 8

Printed and bound in Italy by L.E.G.O. s.p.a., Vicenza

Here are lots of buttons.
Can you sort them into groups?
See how many ways you can do it.

3

You can sort them by colour.

You can sort them by the number of holes.

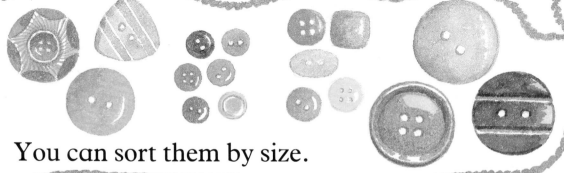

You can sort them by size.

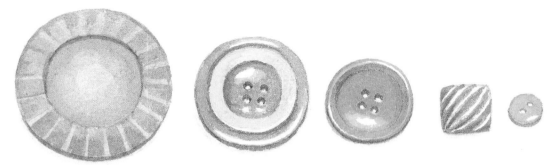

You can put them in order of size.

Find other ways to put them in order.

Anne   Brian   Colin   Debbie

If buttons had names, you could put their
names in order.
You could put them in alphabetical order.

All these animals have names.
Do you know them?
If you do, try to put them into alphabetical
order.

Find an animal beginning with a.
Then find one beginning with b.
All the animals are in alphabetical order on
the next page.

	Bb	**Cc**	**Dd**	**Ee**
Aa ant	butterfly	cat	dog	elephant
	Jj jackal	**Kk** koala	**Ll** llama	**Mm** monkey
	Rr rat	**Ss** snake	**Tt** tapir	**Uu** unicorn

Here are all the animals in alphabetical order.

Ff	Gg	Hh	Ii
frog	gorilla	horse	iguana

Nn	Oo	Pp	Qq
newt	owl	parrot	quail

Vv	Ww	Xx	Yy	Zz
vulture	walrus	x-ray fish	yak	zebra

Think of the names of other animals that begin with a, b, and so on.

The alphabet

Aa apple	**Gg** gloves
Bb balloon	**Hh** hat
Cc candle	**Ii** ice-cream
Dd doll	**Jj** jug
Ee eggs	**Kk** king
Ff flag	**Ll** leaf

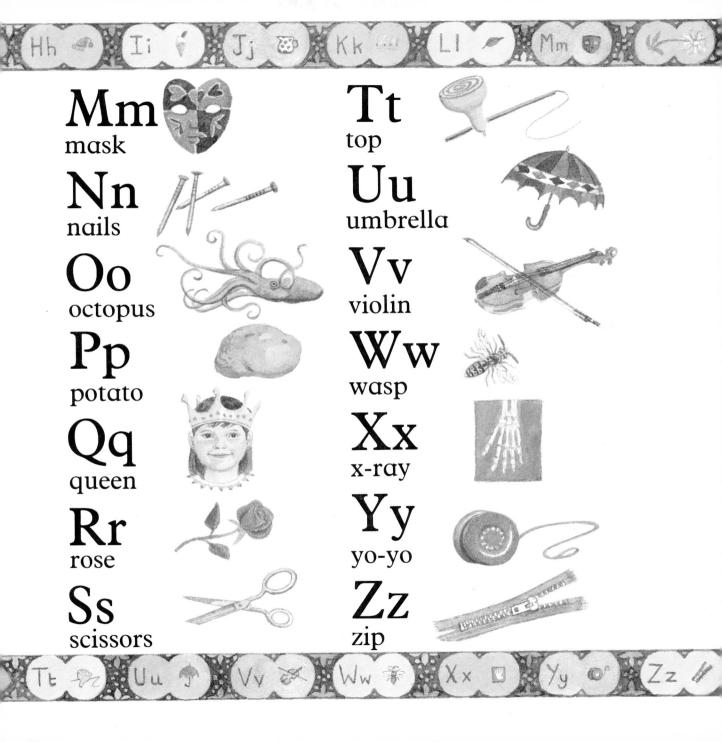

Mm
mask

Nn
nails

Oo
octopus

Pp
potato

Qq
queen

Rr
rose

Ss
scissors

Tt
top

Uu
umbrella

Vv
violin

Ww
wasp

Xx
x-ray

Yy
yo-yo

Zz
zip

Which one of each pair comes first in alphabetical order?

aeroplane

fork

spoon

helicopter

bottle   jug

horse   cow

12   banana   pineapple

Put the animals in these groups into alphabetical order.

giraffe

panda

bear

kangaroo

tiger

wombat

spider

dragonfly

frog

butterfly

ant

tortoise

snake

13

A 🍎 a • b • c • d • e • f • g • h • i • j • k • l • m

Find at least one word for each letter of the alphabet.

sun

kite   cloud   sky

flag

church

ZOO

elephant   ladder   jogger

man   woman

FRUIT   bags

melons

motorbike   boy   girl   plant   hat

oranges   rhubarb

peaches   carrots   bicycle

kiwi fruit   pears   lemons   ice-cream

apples

onions   ribbon

flowers   sack

wheelbarrow

Write the words in alphabetical order.

chimney
nest
bird
factory
houses
bus
yacht
fisherman
rope
lake
swan
reeds
rod
fish
ee
bench
cat
violin
trumpet
kitten
sandwich
quartet
mouse
ukelele
xylophone
drum
dog
hedgehog

Make an alphabet chain

You need:
26 strips of paper (about 16cm × 2cm),
a pen and some glue.

1 Write a different letter of the alphabet on each strip.
2 Stick both ends of strip **a** together.

3 Loop **b** through **a** and glue it.
4 Add all the other links in order until you reach **z**.

5 If you want to wear your chain round your neck, link **z** to **a**.
If you want to hang your chain up, leave the ends free.

Add a word

You need:
7 pieces of card (about 10cm × 10cm),
7 long strips of paper (about 50cm),
strips of paper to write on
(about 4cm deep and 12cm wide), a
pen and some glue.

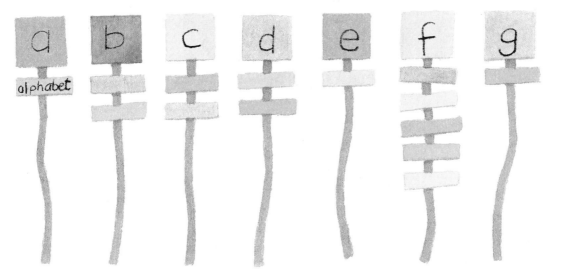

1 Write the letters **a** to **g** on the cards.
2 Glue the long strips to them.
3 Hang them up on the wall.

4 Write words for each letter on the other pieces of paper.
5 Stick them to the long strips.

When you have done **a** to **g**, make some more cards.
Do one strip for each letter of the alphabet.

17

Remember!

Write down the letters of the alphabet in order.
Now look at this picture for two minutes. Then
shut the book.

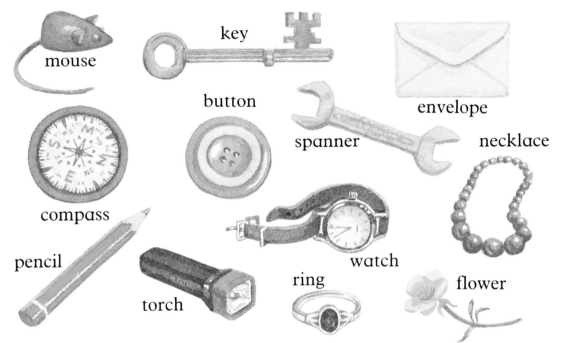

Can you remember the names of all 12 objects?
Write each by its letter on your list.
You can play this game with other objects, with
pictures, or with words written on cards.

I packed my bag

Play this game with your friends.
Say it aloud.

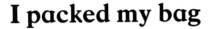

I packed my bag and in it I put an anorak.

I packed my bag and in it I put an anorak and a banana.

I packed my bag and in it I put an anorak, a banana and a camel.

Each player adds a new thing to the list. It must start with the next letter of the alphabet.

More things to do

Keep an alphabet notebook

Put the answers to the questions in it. Think of your own questions and put those in it too.

Keep another notebook with at least one page for each letter of the alphabet. You will need more pages for some letters, such as A, B, C, S and T.

Write new words that you learn in your alphabet notebook.

Looking things up

These are some of the things you find in alphabetical order:

names on a class register
documents in office files
names in a telephone directory
places in a map index
programs on a computer menu
story books in the library (listed under the author's last name)
topics in a book index
words in a dictionary

Make a toy guide

List your toys in alphabetical order, like this: beach ball, castle, chemistry set, cricket bat, doll, frisby . . . List your clothes in the same way.

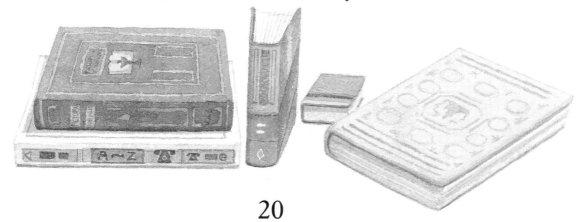

Order your objects

Collect 10 similar objects, such as stones, sweets, buttons and beads. See how many ways you can sort them into order.

Collect 10 model animals or a mixture of objects and put them into order by name.

Draw things in order

Put two headings in your notebook – *first* and *second*. Draw pairs of objects under the headings. Put the cat under *first* and the kitten under *second*.

Make a frieze to go round your room. Draw one object, animal or person for each letter of the alphabet. Try not to use too many of the ones in this book.

Put alphabet cards round your room. Write new words that you like under each letter. Draw pictures of things that you like.

Play 'I Spy'

Players take it in turns to say, 'I spy with my little eye something beginning with . . .', and give a letter. The others have to guess what is spied. The one who guesses becomes the spy.

Collecting words

Write down the alphabet and see if you can think of a kind of fruit or vegetable that begins with each letter – apple, banana, carrot, and so on. Do the same with trees or countries or other groups of things. You will find some letters impossible!

Who has got an A?

This is a game for 2 or more players. Each player has 3 or 4 objects or words written on cards. The leader asks, 'Who has got something beginning with A (then B, C, D and so on)? 'Here's an antelope,' says a player. Players try to be first to get rid of all their objects or words.

1

1 Which letter does your name start with?

2 Find words starting with the first letter of your name on one of the pages of this book.

3 Can you write these letters?
b m p s t w

4 Do you know a word for each letter?

5 Draw a picture for each word.

2

6 Where would you find the page number of a topic in a book?

7 What do we call a book that tells us what words mean?

8 Which of these words will be near the start of a dictionary?
black red yellow white

9 Which of these words will be near the end of a dictionary?
two three five eight

10 What is an encyclopedia?

11 How are the topics in an encyclopedia usually arranged?

12 Which of these topics will be near the front of an encyclopedia?
air stars heat water weather

13 Which of these topics will be in the middle of an encyclopedia?
mountain whale monster cloud sea

3

14 Say all the letters of the alphabet in order without looking. Write them down.

15 Write this list of words in alphabetical order. Use the alphabet at the bottom of a page of this book to help you.

planet air zinnia moon battery needle heat yellow x-ray cough fire oil rock water diamond ice quill juggling telescope violet kite unicorn light gold electricity sand

16 The words on this computer menu should be in alphabetical order. Can you put them in the right order?

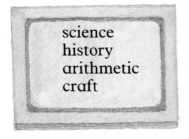

science
history
arithmetic
craft

17 These words are in alphabetical order.
bank beak boat branch building
Can you tell why?

18 How do you put these words into alphabetical order?
ant ape act axe

19 Write a list of your friends' names. See if you can put them into alphabetical order.

20 Find these words in your dictionary and write down their meanings.
thermometer rodent snail cub dagger

21 Look up people with the same last name as yours in the telephone directory.

22 Why are their names listed in the order they are?

Index